mac 2008

Cartoons from the *Daily Mail*

Stan McMurtry **mac**

Edited by Mark Bryant

PORTICO

For Liz, who hides in my cartoons each day and lights up my life.

First published in the United Kingdom in 2008 by
Portico Books
10 Southcombe Street
London
W14 0RA

An imprint of Anova Books Company Ltd

ISBN 9781906032470

A CIP catalogue record for this book is available from the British Library.

10 9 8 7 6 5 4 3 2 1

Typeset by SX Composing DTP, Rayleigh, Essex
Printed and bound by WS Bookwell, Finland

This book can be ordered direct from the publisher.
Contact the marketing department, but try your bookshop first.

www.anovabooks.com

Massive downpours caused chaos, with three months of rain falling in a few hours in some parts of the country. In Tewkesbury, Gloucestershire, flooding left 350,000 people without drinking water when a treatment plant became contaminated.

'Oh, you poor things. How have you managed without drinking water?' *24 July 2007*

A damning report by the Institute for Public Policy Research revealed that Britain's teenagers were the worst-behaved in Europe, and were more likely to binge-drink, take drugs, start fights and have underage sex than their counterparts on the Continent.

'As a change from dominoes, how about us having a night of drink, drugs, violence and sex?' *27 July*

An unprecedented 30,000 junior hospital doctors began work on the same day as a result of the Government's new recruitment process, leading to administrative chaos as well as delays and cancellations in operations such a hip replacements.

1 August

British Airways were accused of acting 'like robbers' and fined a record £270 million by British and US regulators after Virgin Atlantic blew the whistle on their secret agreement on the level of fuel surcharges for passengers on long-haul flights.

'Okay. Keep the engine running.' *2 August*

After it was revealed that 25,000 pieces of luggage had been lost at Heathrow airport during July alone because of staff shortages, British Airways jumbo jets full of missing baggage flew across the Atlantic to try and reduce the backlog.

'That's odd, British Airways said they were in the vicinity and would be dropping off our lost luggage.' *8 August*

A new outbreak of foot-and-mouth virus in Surrey was eventually found by the Department for Environment & Rural Affairs (DEFRA) to have escaped from the Government's own research laboratories in Pirbright near Guildford.

'It's very unusual behaviour. Normally they go out at night and are all back in again by morning.' *9 August*

In the month which marked the 30th anniversary of the death of Elvis Presley – though some believed he was still alive – a retired 62-year-old British photographer who lived in a Land-Rover in North Island, New Zealand, denied that he was Lord Lucan.

'Yeah, man. Turn left at Buddy Holly's place, straight on past Glenn Miller's caravan and Lord Lucan lives on the right.'

10 August

Prime Minister Gordon Brown was criticised for failing to hold a referendum on the treaty on the EU constitution while entering discussions on the proposed referendum on the independence of Scotland from the United Kingdom.

'Shall I put that into the diary, Prime Minister? Fly up to Scotland to vote on their referendum on independence, then return home to refuse one here on the EU treaty.' *15 August*

The Chief Constable of Cheshire blamed feckless parents and called for the legal drinking age to be raised to 21 after a 47-year-old father of three was killed by three drunken youths outside his home in Warrington.

16 August

In an attempt to halt the rising tide of teenage drunkenness, the Government called on supermarkets to act on low alcohol prices and to check the age of purchasers. Meanwhile, A-level results revealed a record pass rate for the tenth successive year.

'I'm terrified to leave the house, too, but someone ought to tell him he's passed his A-levels.' *17 August*

Human Rights lawyers argued that an Italian-born man, who had been released from prison after serving 12 years of a life sentence for murdering headmaster Philip Lawrence while a teenager in Britain, could not be deported to Italy.

'Don't worry about it, gentlemen. Remember it's our human right to be blinkered and stupid.' *22 August*

When 36-year-old BBC TV newsreader Emily Maitlis appeared in a trailer for the 10 O'Clock News perched on the edge of her circular desk there were complaints from viewers who thought she revealed too much of her legs.

'Psst Emily . . . the news. Don't forget to read the news!' *23 August*

A judge in Manchester condemned police for wasting tax-payers' money when it was revealed in court that a 12-year-old boy, who had thrown a cocktail sausage at a pensioner during an argument, had been arrested and charged with common assault.

'Be careful, sarge. He's got a sausage!' *24 August*

Singers Amy Winehouse and Pete Doherty, as well as supermodel Kate Moss, hit the headlines over alleged drugtaking. Meanwhile, official figures revealed that opium poppy production in Afghanistan had reached record levels, accounting for 93% of the world's total.

'It's probably to celebrate the bumper poppy crop in Afghanistan.' *29 August*

After much speculation the Duchess of Cornwall did not attend the memorial service to mark the tenth anniversary of the death of Princess Diana. Meanwhile, the *New Scientist* reported that South Korean researchers had discovered that plants do react to music and other sounds.

'. . . so I said "Come on, old gel. Don't fly off on your own. Come to the memorial." "Not bloody likely," she said. "Why not?" I said. "I'll tell you why not!" she said, lobbing a plate at my head . . .' *31 August*

In a highly controversial move, the Human Fertilisation & Embryology Authority gave the go-ahead to the production of part-human, part-animal embryos known as 'chimeras' to help research into Parkinson's, Alzheimer's and other incurable diseases.

'... and so, having participated in extensive tests, we see no reason why human-animal chimera research should not proceed...' *4 September*

Education Secretary Ed Balls announced a new initiative to give all secondary-school children lessons in happiness and emotional well-being despite reports from the Institute of Education that they did little to improve attendance or reduce exclusions.

'Dear teacher. Thank you for yesterday's truly inspirational lesson which has changed our lives – we're all down at the pub.'

5 September

Research published in *The Lancet* by scientists working for the Government's Food Standards Agency found that artificial additives in children's food – especially colourings in sweets, biscuits, soft drinks and ice-cream – can affect their behaviour.

'That was delicious, mummy. Don't worry, I'll do the dishes, then I think I'll tidy my room and curl up in bed with my book on Scouting.' *7 September*

In an official report for the Home Office, Chief Inspector of Constabulary Sir Ronnie Flanagan said that his investigations had revealed that today's police were too bogged down in paperwork and bureaucracy to do their jobs properly.

'All right, all right, constable. It's a deal. I'll come round and help you with your paperwork if you'll help me with my burglary.'

13 September

In his opening speech at the Labour Party conference in Bournemouth – his first as leader – Gordon Brown pledged to introduce a 'deep clean' programme for all wards in NHS hospitals in an attempt to eradicate superbugs.

'Okay, Mrs Henderson. As soon as you've finished your bed space it's bathies time.' *25 September*

Later in the Bournemouth conference, Health Secretary Alan Johnson added that hospitals would face fines if they failed to improve hygiene standards. Meanwhile, an exhibition of some of China's famous Terracotta Army figures opened at the British Museum.

'The one in the middle was found by archaeologists under the dirt when a local hospital was cleaned.' *26 September*

A new poll conducted for Channel 4 News gave Labour an eleven-point lead over the Conservatives, fuelling speculation that Gordon Brown would call an election in November.

'For heaven's sake, Gordon. Stop dithering and call an election. I want to know if I can unpack!' *27 September*

Secretary Jack Straw proposed an amendment to the Criminal Justice & Immigration Bill to allow citizens to use 'reasonable force' in self-defence against burglars and other criminals.

'You fool! The violence my husband is about to administer comes with the full authority of Jack Straw.' *28 September*

Speaking at the Conservative Party conference in Blackpool, Shadow Chancellor George Osborne promised that a Tory government would revise the law on inheritance tax so that only estates worth more than £1 million would be liable.

'Sorry to have bothered you. We have persuaded grandad not to go until the Tories get back in again.' *2 October*

As the long-awaited inquest into the death of Princess Diana and Dodi Fayed opened at the High Court in London there was speculation that the Queen herself might be called to give evidence. (Dame Helen Mirren had won an Oscar for her film portrayal of the Queen.)

'Hello. Dame Helen Mirren? I wonder if you'd do me a huge favour?' *3 October*

Prime Minister Gordon Brown pledged that half of Britain's GPs would be made to open their surgeries on Saturday mornings or on at least one evening during the working week within the next three years.

'Because this is what I normally do on a Saturday morning, that's why – now open wide!' *5 October*

In the Queen's Speech at the opening of Parliament it was revealed that the school leaving age was to be raised to 18 and that parents would have a legal duty to keep children in education or training until that age or face fines.

'Pay attention, class. Due to a Government ruling you'll be playing truant for another two years.' *7 November*

After the London Assembly passed a vote of no confidence in him, Metropolitan Police Commissioner Sir Ian Blair faced renewed calls for his resignation over the shooting of an innocent Brazilian man mistaken for a terrorist at Stockwell Underground station.

'Please help me! I'm an innocent police chief being chased by crazy people trying to finish me off!' *8 November*

A Nottingham mother who had booked a man in a gorilla suit to turn up in a drama class at her son's school as a 16th birthday surprise was stunned when a female stripper dressed as a policewoman appeared instead and performed an erotic dance act.

'Before I go I'd like to apologise for any disappointment caused by the man in the gorilla suit not turning up.' *9 November*

Leaked documents revealed that Home Secretary Jacqui Smith had sent secret memos to try and cover up a report by the Security Industry Authority that at least 5000 illegal immigrants had been cleared to work in sensitive Whitehall security jobs.

'Yes, mistakes have been made regarding illegal immigrants and jobs in security, but rest assured we are leaving no stone unturned . . .' *14 November*

A new outbreak of bird flu – which has killed 300 people worldwide since 2003 – was confirmed at a turkey farm in Norfolk. Meanwhile, an exhibition of 3000-year-old artefacts from the tomb of the Egyptian boy-king Tutankhamun opened in London.

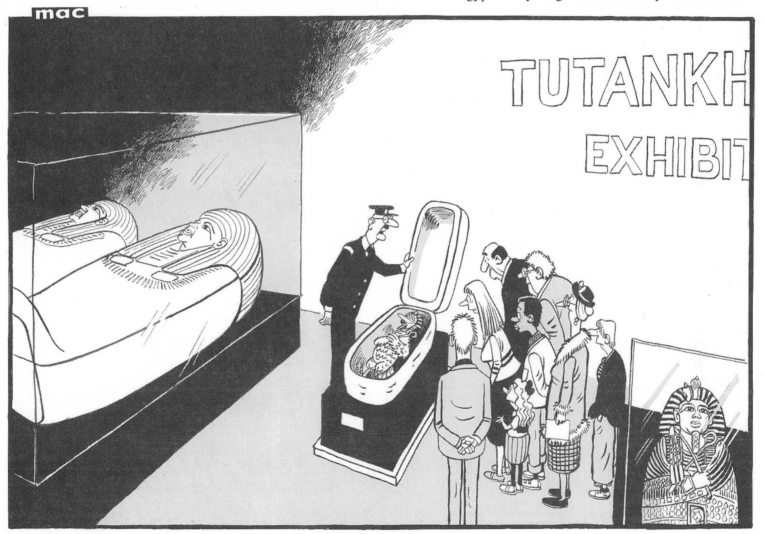

'. . . and this is the sacred gilded turkey which sneezed on Tutankhamun just before it was going to be dinner.' *15 November*

The Government announced that from 2009 onwards security officials would require all those entering or leaving Britain to provide 53 pieces of personal information, including credit-card details, email addresses and holiday contact numbers.

'Have a nice holiday. Remember it's advisable to get to the airport two days before take-off.' *16 November*

The controversial Human Fertilisation & Embryology Bill, which would allow lesbian couples to have children by IVF treatment and be regarded as their joint legal parents, was hotly debated in Parliament.

'There's something I've got to tell you, lads . . .I'm gay, I'm female and I'm pregnant.' *20 November*

When Chancellor Alistair Darling admitted that two HM Revenue & Customs computer discs containing personal and banking details of 25 million Child Benefit claimants had gone missing in the post there were nationwide worries about the risk of identity fraud.

'Good heavens, Mavis. It's you! This woman must have stolen your identity!' *22 November*

As it was announced that the sacked England football manager, Steve McLaren, would receive a £2.5 million payoff, it was revealed that the outgoing chief executive of the failed bank Northern Rock would also receive a massive severance package.

'Failed football manager, eh? What a coincidence. I'm the failed head of Northern Rock.' *23 November*

Sir Richard Branson's Virgin Group emerged as the hot favourite to take over the stricken Newcastle-based mortgage bank, Northern Rock.

'Well, she won't last long up here.' *27 November*

Labour's General Secretary Peter Watt resigned after admitting that he had known that multi-millionaire property tycoon David Abrahams had given the party nearly £400,000 in secret donations using middlemen.

'No more secrecy about donations then.' *28 November*

Sleaze allegations continued to dog Gordon Brown when it was revealed that Harriet Harman had accepted £5000 from David Abrahams to help fund her campaign to become Deputy Leader of the Labour Party.

'Oh. You're home early, Gordon, darling – how was your day?' *29 November*

A report by the Family Education Trust revealed that girls as young as 12 are able to obtain 'morning after' pills from chemists' shops without their parents' knowledge.

'Thank you for a lovely party. I really enjoyed myself – will you remind Jennifer to take her morning-after pill?' *4 December*

After a 57-year-old Hartlepool man who had been presumed dead after disappearing during a canoeing trip in the North Sea turned up at a police station, his wife was arrested in Panama City on suspicion of being involved with a life-insurance scam.

'Ah, Miss Binks. Get my widow on the phone, give her my sincere condolences and tell her the airline tickets are on the bedside table.' *6 December*

To help solve the problem of Britain's overcrowded prisons Lord Carter, the Government's adviser on the issue, proposed that fewer low-risk criminals should be jailed, advocating electronic tags and community service as an alternative.

'First they stopped us hanging people, then we were told not to jail anyone, then gradually we became superfluous.' *7 December*

61-year-old Italian Fabio Capello took over as England's new football manager. A notoriously hard taskmaster, he vowed to shake up the team's playboy millionaires and impose stricter discipline on its more wayward members.

'Hey, Rooney. Da boss he say eet's 6.30. Why you not in bed?' *14 December*

It was revealed that the Home Office's Voluntary Assisted Return Programme for failed asylum-seekers, launched in 1999, had so far resulted in 23,000 people being offered £4000 each to return and open businesses in their homelands.

'It was well worth the trip. I got an ostrich farm and my wife got a beauty salon near Tehran.' *18 December*

In an attempt to improve his English by the time of his team's match with Switzerland in February, England manager Fabio Capello signed up for lessons at a school specialising in football vocabulary.

'Enunciate man, enunciate! Okay, try again . . . Pass the f****** ball, you stupid p****! Oy, ref! 'Ave you left your *f* ****** specs at 'ome?' *19 December*

'That's the last Manchester United party I go to – they treat you like a piece of meat.' *20 December*

The Crown Prosecution Service announced that under tough new rules drivers caught using hand-held devices such as mobile phones could be jailed for up to two years.

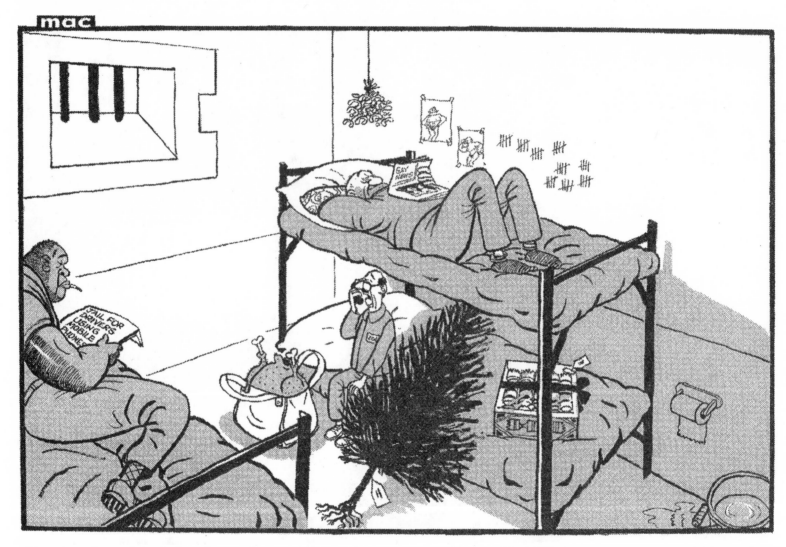

'Yes, dear. I've got the turkey, the crackers and the tree. I was on my way home with them when you rang earlier.' *21 December*

'Aw. Bless him. Our Wayne's sticking to his New Year's resolution – he hasn't touched one chocolate.' *1 January 2008*

Gordon Brown's proposed new NHS 'contract' to protect patients' rights would also include a general requirement for people to keep themselves fit, warning that smokers, drinkers and the obese could risk losing NHS care.

'Keep up, keep up! Only another two miles to the hospital . . . hup, two, three, four . . .' *2 January*

When a 68-year-old animal behaviourist from East Sussex developed crippling arthritis in her back, she trained her Newfoundland dog to work the washing-machine, help with housework and carry shopping bags.

'... and another thing. Next door's dog does the laundry, tidies up and brings the shopping home!' *4 January*

The Prime Minister announced that the Government would be introducing a free annual 'health MOT' for every adult in Britain – the world's first ever national screening programme for heart disease, strokes and diabetes.

'I'm sorry, Mr Perkins. Your wife has failed her MOT – do you want her fixed or will you get a new one?' *8 January*

In his Channel 4 television series, *Jamie's Fowl Dinners*, Jamie Oliver continued his crusade to improve the welfare of chickens by showing gruesome footage of how the birds are killed in battery farms.

'Okay. Come and get me! I don't want to go the way that Jamie Oliver describes.' *10 January*

The Business Secretary, John Hutton, announced that the Government had given the go-ahead for the building of a new generation of nuclear power stations which would be in place 'well before 2020'.

'We'll soon have it nice and warm in here . . . the Government have only just given the OK to go nuclear.' *11 January*

Gordon Brown backed plans to allow transplant surgeons to remove organs from dead patients without their prior consent unless family members objected. Meanwhile, Work & Pensions Secretary, Peter Hain, faced the sack over secret funding of his failed bid for the deputy leadership.

'I'm not going to sack you, Peter. But I've decided to donate a few of your organs to science.' *15 January*

After admitting that she did not feel safe walking the streets of London after dark, Home Secretary Jacqui Smith tried to make amends by saying that she had bought a kebab one evening in Peckham. It was later revealed that she had had a police escort.

'Please stop screaming, Home Secretary. The man in the shop is supposed to have a knife.' *22 January*

Schools Secretary Ed Balls announced that all secondary-school pupils aged between 11 and 14 would be given practical cookery lessons in an effort to combat obesity and to encourage teenagers to eat healthy meals instead of relying on processed foods.

'You were asked to bring two sardines and a carrot, Munshmore. Giant beefburgers and chips are out.' *23 January*

In Britain's largest ever police demonstration, more than 22,000 rank-and-file officers marched through London after the Home Secretary, Jacqui Smith, refused to honour the findings of an independent arbitration tribunal over their pay.

'Oh my God, Bernard. I told you not to park on a double yellow line!' *24 January*

After a study suggested that 60% of Britain's population would be obese by 2050, the Government proposed introducing vouchers for fat people to spend on healthy food and cash prizes for those who managed to lose weight.

'**Doris, we need some money to pay the gas bill – have you ever heard of liposuction?**' *25 January*

A senior Tory MP was suspended after it was revealed that he had paid his 22-year-old son £45,000 of taxpayers' money, claiming that he was working as his father's parliamentary assistant, when in reality he was a student living in Newcastle.

'Has the man no shame? My parliamentary assistant is not in the family and earns every penny he gets . . . don't you, Archie?'

30 January

A survey conducted by the *Daily Mail* revealed that 63 MPs admitted to employing relatives to help them with their parliamentary business.

'In view of current investigations I'm afraid I can no longer keep you on as my parliamentary assistant, mother.' *31 January*

As the row over MPs' expenses continued, it was reported that a senior Muslim Labour MP had been bugged by police, in a clear breach of parliamentary rules.

5 February

Despite the fact that a large piece of Buckingham Palace masonry had nearly hit Princess Anne last summer, the Government turned down the Queen's request for an additional £3 million to repair her crumbling royal residences.

'Damned cheek! No money for Palace repairs – only a note from Brown saying, "You can do it if you B & Q it."' *8 February*

The divorce hearing between multimillionaire ex-Beatle Sir Paul McCartney and his second wife, Heather Mills, opened in the High Court in London.

'Final question, Miss Mills. Should you acquire a substantial amount of Sir Paul's assets, would you make a lonely old bachelor extremely happy?' *12 February*

The Government were accused of policing 'on the cheap' when a leaked memo suggested that Neighbourhood Watch members should be asked to patrol streets, check road-tax discs and perform other tasks normally carried out by police officers.

'I worry about him. Sometimes he's out for hours in the cold doing his Neighbourhood Watch patrol.' *13 February*

As St Valentine's Day dawned there was speculation that the ongoing McCartney-Mills divorce case would result in a record-breaking settlement.

'Eat your heart out, Heather Mills. I bet she won't be getting a romantic new dishmop from Sir Paul.' *14 February*

The Government announced trials of a 'Find Your Talent' scheme in which school children would spend up to five hours a week in visits to theatres, galleries and museums. Meanwhile, police chiefs attacked the drinks industry for selling beer 'cheaper than water'.

'That's right, mate. Theatres, museums, galleries and off-licences. All part of New Labour's five hours of culture initiative.'

15 February

Four Greenpeace environmental protesters managed to climb onto a British Airways Boeing 777 and attach a banner to its tail in a major security breach at Heathrow airport.

'Do we want any duty-frees?' *26 February*

As the Speaker of the House of Commons became the latest to face scrutiny over alleged false expenses claims, MPs debated awarding themselves a massive 33% pay-rise. Meanwhile, new research claimed that anti-depressants such as Prozac did not work.

'Who needs pills? I find this stuff always cheers me up.' *27 February*

Britain's second-largest earthquake in the past decade, measuring 4.7 on the Richter scale, shook most of England from Durham to the Home Counties.

'Honestly. I'd just finished tidying my room when there was this huge earth tremor.' *28 February*

23-year-old Prince Harry was forced to cut short his tour of duty with the British Army in Afghanistan when news of his secret deployment was leaked and he became a potential target for terrorists.

'I know it's out of season, Benskin. But the poor lad's really missing all the action in Afghanistan.' *4 March*

As Hillary Clinton and Barack Obama battled it out to become Democratic candidate in the US Presidential elections, the British public were finally denied a say on the EU constitution when MPs voted against holding a referendum on the Lisbon Treaty.

'**Leadership is different in the UK, honey. A guy struggles to the top then happily hands over all the decisions to some other guys in Brussels.**' *6 March*

The *Daily Mail* began a campaign to ban free throwaway plastic carrier-bags in supermarkets, which blight the countryside and block waterways. Before long most of Britain's retailers – including the largest, Tesco – had joined the campaign.

'**Remember. If anyone asks, just say we're part of the "Ban Plastic Bags campaign".**' *7 March*

Chancellor of the Exchequer Alistair Darling prepared his first Budget, the first one in a decade to be written in close consultation with No.10.

'Don't be so impatient, Alistair. You'll get to read it on Wednesday.' *11 March*

Gas-guzzling cars faced being taxed off the road by the Budget, with 4x4s and sports cars having to pay up to £950 in road tax for the first year. Duty on alcohol also rose dramatically by 6% above the rate of inflation.

'Welcome to your green stretch-limo service, ladies. The booze is in the back – let's party!' *14 March*

At the close of her divorce battle with Sir Paul McCartney, Heather Mills was awarded £24.3 million. Meanwhile, the City reeled after one of the worst trading days for years as bank share-values plummeted and the FTSE fell to its lowest level since 2005.

May I suggest, Lady McCartney, that until the economy settles down a bit one splashes out on a nice big safe?' *19 March*

'Listen carefully, Peregrine, old chap. I'm telling you this in the strictest confidence . . . ' *21 March*

Air passengers faced a summer of chaos when the new £4.3 million British Airways-only Terminal 5 at Heathrow airport finally opened. Hundreds of flights were cancelled and thousands of bags were lost.

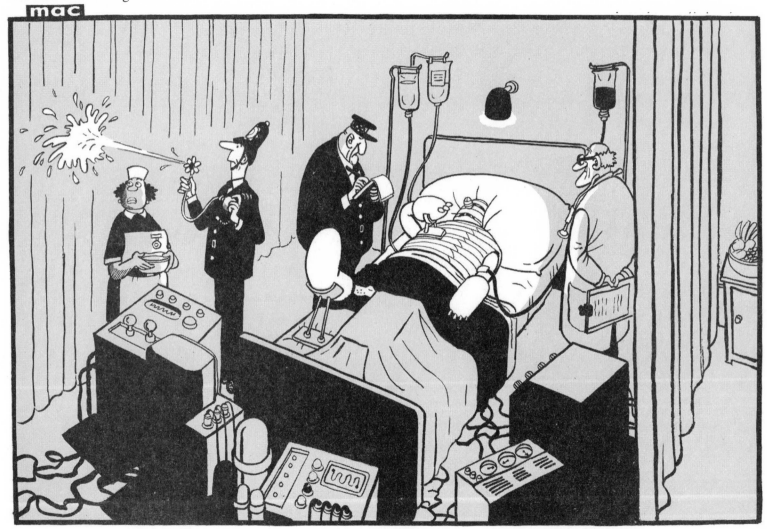

'I see, sir. You work at Terminal 5 and to cheer people up you gave them a merry little squirt with your joke flower before saying: "April Fool. Your flight's been cancelled . . . ".' *1 April*

41-year-old Lib Dem leader Nick Clegg revealed in an interview for *GQ* magazine that he had had 'no more than 30' sexual partners but added: 'It's a lot less than that.'

'Normally politicians just ask for your support – but wowee! Not that Nick Clegg!' *2 April*

Scientists at Newcastle University created the first ever part-human, part-animal embryo by inserting human skin cells into the egg cells of a cow.

'Mummy. I'd like you to meet Kevin . . .' *3 April*

The inquest into the deaths of Princess Diana and Dodi Fayed concluded that it had been an accident, though Mohammed Al Fayed remained convinced that Prince Philip and MI6 had been involved. Meanwhile, as the Olympic flame reached San Francisco, pro-Tibet demonstrators unfurled a banner on the Golden Gate bridge.

'Gee. Doesn't that guy Al Fayed ever give up?' *9 April*

Reports by the Royal Institution of Chartered Surveyors and others revealed that the housing market was at its worst for 30 years with one in three estate agents facing closure within the next twelve months.

'Oh yes. I come down here most mornings to feed the estate agents.' *15 April*

A survey by an online research company revealed that the cost of basic foods had rocketed and that the average household shopping bill was likely to increase by £600 this year, with the price of chicken up 70% and beef up 64%.

'Peas and chips again? Surely there's some meat in the house we can eat?' *16 April*

In what RAF chiefs later insisted was a 'legitimate training' exercise Prince William flew a £10 million Chinook transport helicopter to the Isle of Wight to attend a stag party for his cousin Peter Philips, stopping in London en route to pick up his brother Harry.

'Isn't that kind, dear? William popped in on his way to a party and offered to walk the corgis.' *17 April*

As the NHS dentists' crisis deepened – with half of Britain's population now without an NHS dentist – shocking new figures revealed a 20% increase in hospital dental admissions and widespread reports of patients resorting to DIY dental treatment.

'I might be a bit late home, luv. I've got a radicular canal filling of the upper lateral incisor to do afterwards.' *18 April*

In an unprecedented move, the Bank of England revealed plans to pump £50 billion of taxpayers' money into the financial system in an effort to halt the threatened mortgage meltdown.

'Hang on. I think I may be able to help you with a mortgage after all.' *22 April*

A court ordered a 26-year-old father-of-four to pay a £210 fine or face imprisonment after a local council enforcement officer found that he had illegally overfilled his wheelie bin by four inches.

'I'm so proud of him. After he's rid the country of wheelie-bin offenders, he's planning to invade Poland.' *23 April*

One in three schools faced closure after members of the National Union of Teachers took part
in the first national teachers' strike in 21 years over a below-inflation pay offer.

**'Teachers! Who needs them? You play truant for months and the very day you decide to pop in for some education what do the
workshy layabouts do . . .?'** *24 April*

A report by the consumer watchdog group Which? claimed that 10% of food is not what it seems, with inferior foods being dressed up as top-quality products. Examples included 'free-range' eggs, 'organic' meat, 'wild' fish and 'extra virgin' olive oil.

'Try to merge in. I think we're being marketed as venison.' *25 April*

A 73-year-old Austrian man was arrested after keeping his daughter locked in the cellar of his house for 24 years. Meanwhile, the memoirs of former Labour Party fund-raiser, Lord Levy, claimed that Tony Blair had been given 'long massages' by former topless model Carole Caplin while Prime Minister.

'Answer the question, Tony! How long have you had Carole Caplin locked in our cellar?' *29 April*

Oil companies were accused of profiteering as the cost of crude oil reached a record high of $120 a barrel. As a result, soaring petrol prices broke through the £5-a-gallon (£1.10-a-litre) barrier and analysts predicted they would reach £1.50 a litre by the autumn.

'Wonderful news, darling . . .somebody's stolen the car!' *30 April*

After it was revealed that prisoners were to receive a 37.5% pay rise, Gordon Brown stepped in to delay the increase, pending further review. Meanwhile, news leaked that drugs and even prostitutes were being smuggled in to some so-called 'cushy jails'.

'I don't know how they got out, Prime Minister. But they have and they've got a petition.' *1 May*

A man who lost the top of his finger after an accident claimed to have regrown it completely using 'pixie dust' made from dried pig's bladder. Meanwhile, Labour had its worst election result in 40 years, losing more than 300 local council seats.

'Gosh, Gordon. So many people showing how they've regrown fingers with that magic powder.' *2 May*

To add to Gordon Brown's electoral misery, Tory Boris Johnson defeated Labour's Ken Livingstone to become Mayor of London. Meanwhile, former premier Tony Blair bought a £4 million stately home in Buckinghamshire once owned by actor Sir John Gielgud.

6 May

A report by insurance companies revealed that thefts from gardens had doubled over the past twelve months. As well as statues and garden furniture, expensive plants, trees, shrubs and even whole lawns had been uprooted.

'Keep a close eye on my azaleas. Apparently garden thefts are on the increase.' *7 May*

As the Government announced that it planned to build three million new homes by 2020, a report by the Campaign to Protect Rural England claimed that 30,000 acres of Green Belt protected land around cities had been lost since Labour came to power.

'Mrs Higgins from the flats next door says can she borrow a cup of sugar till she's been down the shops?' *8 May*

As a poll reported that 55% of Labour voters thought Gordon Brown should quit, Scottish Labour Party Leader Wendy Alexander defied the Prime Minister's official stance and called for a referendum on Scotland's independence from the UK.

'I've tried, I really have. But does anyone seriously believe in Gordon Brown?' *9 May*

Two new autobiographies by Labour Party insiders – *Prezza, My Story* by former Deputy Prime Minister John Prescott and Cherie Blair's *Speaking for Myself* – portrayed Gordon Brown in a negative light during his years as Chancellor.

'I suppressed a whimper of anticipation as he tore off his clothes revealing his fine toned, rippling torso . . .with one bound he was by my side, breathing into my ear his plans for the Crewe by-election . . .' *13 May*

Other revelations from Cherie Blair's memoirs included the admission that their son Leo had been conceived in 1999 during the annual Prime Minister's trip to Balmoral Castle in Scotland as guests of the Queen and Prince Philip.

'Don't worry, ma'am. We've tested it out. There will be no more "conceiving" in the guest bedroom.' *14 May*

Details of 7000 sightings of unidentified flying objects logged by the Ministry of Defence and published online by the National Archives revealed that they reached a peak shortly after the release of Steven Spielberg's film *Close Encounters of the Third Kind* (1978).

'I hope we haven't over-reacted. This thing he stuck on the side might be a welcome note.' *15 May*

Tables compiled by the International Association for the Study of Obesity showed that Scottish and English women are the fattest in Europe. Meanwhile, a portrait of a naked obese woman by Lucien Freud became the world's most expensive painting by a living artist when it sold for £17.2 million.

'Me too. I want to be a model and get discovered by Lucian Freud.' *16 May*

In a landmark decision the Human Fertilisation & Embryology Bill was passed by Parliament, giving the official go-ahead for the creation of animal-human embryos – banned in 21 other countries and criticised as 'monstrous' by the Roman Catholic Church.

'I'd like a fiver on the horse from the animal-human embryo research lab.' *20 May*

MPs voted to scrap the need for doctors to consider the presence of a father or male role model as a precondition for women seeking IVF treatment. Meanwhile, local councils introduced tougher penalties for those putting out the 'wrong' type of rubbish.

'Sorry, love. Unwanted fathers go in the yellow bags.' *21 May*

Buckingham Palace officials objected when unapproved photographs of senior members of the royal family appeared in *Hello!* magazine's coverage of the marriage of Princess Anne's son Peter Philips in St George's Chapel, Windsor.

'The centrefold editor of *Playboy* magazine on the phone for you, ma'am.' *22 May*

Forecasters predicted a 'summer of misery' for motorists as the price of oil continued to rise and there were calls for the Government to reduce the tax on petrol.

"Oy! Where are these b***** children? I've been here 15 minutes now!'** *23 May*

In the face of increases in the cost of food, gas, electricity and petrol, rebel Labour MPs backed a Commons motion to reconsider plans to introduce higher road taxes on large family cars, seeing this as a recipe for political disaster.

'. . . saturate with juice of motorist . . .' *28 May*

As millions struggled to cope with soaring living costs and police, nurses and teachers received below-inflation wage-rises, MPs demanded an extra £38,000 a year in lieu of expenses – giving them an average annual salary of £100,000.

'They didn't have time for dessert: they're discussing their expenses and pay-rises.' *29 May*

There were calls for the BBC to sack *Top Gear* presenter Jeremy Clarkson when he admitted in an interview that he had driven a car at 186mph on a public road.

'Okay, let her down . . . slowly . . . slowly . . .hang on, Fred. Jeremy Clarkson's coming up. See if you can get his autograph.'

30 May

In an attempt to curb teenage binge-drinking Chief Medical Officer Sir Liam Donaldson introduced a Youth Alcohol Action Plan which laid out new guidelines for parents regarding the consumption of alcohol by children at home.

'Personally, I think 42 days' detention without charge on suspicion of two alcopops is a bit harsh.' *3 June*

Interviewed in the *Sun*, General Sir Richard Dannatt, head of the British Army, called for pay-rises for his soldiers, many of whom earnt less than traffic-wardens even though they risked their lives for their country in wars.

'Yes, sir. It's me, Private Jones . . . I had no idea traffic-wardens earn so much.' *6 June*

As details emerged of huge expenses claims by Conservative Euro MPs Tory leader David Cameron announced a 'zero tolerance' approach to the misuse of public funds.

'They just love watching programmes where crooks steal thousands of pounds then get away with it.' *10 June*

Motorists were urged not to panic-buy petrol as fuel-tanker drivers proposed to launch a four-day strike over an unsatisfactory pay-rise offer by employers.

'No, no, don't go yet. Just one more . . .have you heard the one about the Irishman, the nun and the one-legged parrot?' *12 June*

A salesman from Buckinghamshire began a £100,000-a-year job with Sir Alan Sugar after winning BBC 1's *The Apprentice*. Meanwhile a Government report criticised Britain's unemployed for failing to take up jobs now filled by immigrants from Eastern Europe.

'It was a bit far-fetched – more than a dozen people all trying to get something called a job.' *13 June*

Allegations made in the *News of the World* that Paul Burrell had boasted to his brother-in-law that he had had regular sex with Princess Diana were strenuously denied by the former royal butler.

'I still have my memories. But that cad, Paul Burrell . . . he never phones, he never writes.' *17 June*

The Government abandoned its 'chip-in-bin' electronic waste-charging system as the 'pay-as-you-throw' technology had failed and trials had led to a 250% increase in fly-tipping. Meanwhile, the annual Royal Ascot horseracing event opened in Berkshire.

'Okay. Nobody's looking – fly-tip it behind the stewards' enclosure.' *18 June*

A court in the oil-rich African state of Equatorial Guinea sought to extradite Sir Mark Thatcher, son of the former Conservative Prime Minister, Lady Thatcher, for his alleged involvement in a failed coup to topple the country's government in 2004.

'It's all right, Mark, dear. It's only Mummy. Would you like a nice cup of tea?' *20 June*

Robert Mugabe, President of Zimbabwe for the past 28 years, was returned to power after escalating violence against supporters of Morgan Tsvangirai, leader of the Movement for Democratic Change, forced him to withdraw from the final stages of the election.

24 June

The annual Wimbledon lawn tennis tournament began in London. Meanwhile, the housing crisis continued with many having their homes repossessed for defaulting on their mortgage repayments.

'At the end of this game I think we should break it to your mother that the house has been repossessed.' *26 June*

The Information Commissioner condemned Government plans to introduce a massive database snooping on the entire population – detailing phone calls, emails, text messages, internet searches and online purchases in its fight against terrorism – as a 'step too far'.

'Attention, attention! The Government database cannot fight terror if you mumble . . . please speak slowly and distinctly . . .'

17 July

After millions of SATs exam papers were discovered to have been incompetently marked there were fears that many pupils would have to resit them. Meanwhile, the Government banned 'happy hours' and 'supersize' wine glasses in pubs and bars to try and reduce teenage alcohol problems.

'Have you no compassion? They're going to lose happy hour, put up with small measures and on top of that resit their SATs exams.' *22 July*

In an effort to end Britain's 'sick-note culture' Work & Pensions Secretary James Purnell announced plans to scrap incapacity benefit and to offer two million claimants 'back-to-work' grants to take up jobs.

'Dammit, Marjorie. This new butler you've taken on is terribly slow!' *23 July*

34-year-old Welsh-born actor, Christian Bale, who stars as Batman in the new blockbuster *The Dark Knight*, was arrested by police after he had allegedly assaulted his mother at the Dorchester Hotel shortly before the film's London premiere.

'Take your time. We have to be absolutely sure. Which is the man you think assaulted you?' *24 July*

The *News of the World* was ordered to pay a record £60,000 in a breach-of-privacy case for reporting that Formula 1 motor-racing chief Max Mosley, son of British Fascist leader Oswald Mosley, had allegedly indulged in a 'sick Nazi orgy' with five prostitutes.

'I don't understand . . . you used to hate motor sports.' *25 July*

Carol Vorderman resigned as co-presenter of Channel 4's *Countdown* show after 26 years when she was told that her £800,000-a-year salary would be cut by 90%. Meanwhile, during Gordon Brown's holiday in Southwold, Suffolk, there were more calls for his resignation.

'Great news, Gordon. They're looking for someone who's cheap and reasonable at sums to replace Carol Vorderman on *Countdown*.' *29 July*

A 900-word article published in the *Guardian*, which set out Foreign Secretary David Miliband's personal manifesto for beating the Tories, was seen by many to be preparing the ground for a Labour leadership battle.

'Show some respect, man! With all the plotting who knows who might be Prime Minister next?' *31 July*

61-year old television presenter Chris Tarrant, a keen angler, was photographed reading *Trout and Salmon* magazine while sunbathing on a yacht in Spain with his 45-year-old girlfriend Jane Bird.

'A penny for your thoughts, Chris.' *6 August*

Damning statistics emerged about Britain's filthy NHS hospitals, with widespread reports of infestation by rats, mice, cockroaches, ants, fleas, bedbugs and maggots adding to the danger from deadly superbugs such as MRSA.

'Don't worry. We'll find your husband soon. We think we know where the nest is.' *7 August*

Despite concerns from athletes and officials over smog and high levels of humidity in Beijing, the Olympic torch was lit in the main Bird's Nest Stadium near the Great Wall of China at the start of a spectacular opening ceremony.

'Getting lost in the smog doesn't worry me. It's the bloke behind I feel sorry for.' *8 August*